This selection of quotations comes from the letters and teachings of St Paul.

Written originally to the early churches during times of personal joy and frustration, triumph and defeat, they contain much treasured wisdom which lies at the heart of the Christian gospel.

Each quotation is illustrated with a graphic, contemporary image and includes a hidden insight and words of wisdom beneath the extra leaf on each page.

I N S I G H T S

FROM · THE · WORDS · OF · ST · PAUL

A LION BOOK

Tring • Batavia • Sydney

THE WAY TO GOD

God in his wisdom made it impossible for people to know him by means of their own wisdom . . . God purposely chose what the world considers weak in order to shame the powerful. He chose what the world looks down on and despises in order to destroy what the world thinks is important. This means that no one can boast in God's presence.

O the depth of the riches and wisdom
and knowledge of God!
How unsearchable are his judgments
and how inscrutable his ways!

F ORGIVENESS

Jews and Gentiles alike are all under the power of sin. As the Scriptures say:

'There is no one who is righteous, no one who is wise or who worships God. All have turned away from God; they have all gone wrong; no one does what is right, not even one . . .'

Everyone has sinned
and is far away from God's saving presence.
But by the free gift of God's grace
all are put right with him
through Christ Jesus, who sets them free.

GOOD NEWS

I have complete confidence in the gospel; it is God's power to save all those who believe . . . For the gospel reveals how God puts people right with himself; it is through faith from beginning to end.

The wages of sin is death,
but the gift of God is eternal life
in Christ Jesus.

E QUALITY

In the Lord woman is not independent of man, nor is man independent of woman. For as woman came from man, so also man is born of woman.

There is neither Jew nor Greek,
slave nor free, male nor female,
for all are one in Christ Jesus.

R A C I S M

For there is no difference between Jew and Gentile. The same Lord is Lord of all and richly blesses all who call on him for 'Everyone who calls on the name of the Lord will be saved.'

Christ himself has brought us peace by making Jews and Gentiles one people. With his own body he broke down the wall that separated them and kept them enemies . . .

By his death on the cross Christ destroyed their enmity; by means of the cross he united both races into one body and brought them back to God.

CONTENTMENT

Godliness with contentment is great gain. For we brought nothing into the world, and we can take nothing out of it. If we have food and clothing, we should be content with that. People who want to get rich fall into temptation and a trap and into many foolish and harmful desires that plunge people into ruin and destruction. For the love of money is a root of all kinds of evil.

And God is able to provide you
with every blessing in abundance, so that
you may always have enough of everything
and may provide in abundance
for every good work.

P EACEMAKING

Do not repay anyone evil for evil. Be careful to do what is right
in the eyes of everybody. If it is possible, as far as it depends on
you, live at peace with everyone. Do not take revenge . . . but
leave room for God's wrath, for it is written, 'It is mine to
avenge; I will repay,' says the Lord.

If your enemy is hungry, feed him;
if he is thirsty, give him something to drink.
In doing this, you will heap burning
coals on his head.
Do not be overcome by evil;
but overcome evil with good.

L O V E

Love is patient, love is kind. It does not envy, it does not boast, it is not proud. It is not rude, it is not self-seeking, it is not easily angered, it keeps no record of wrongs. Love does not delight in evil but rejoices with the truth. It always protects, always trusts, always hopes, always perseveres.

Faith, hope and love abide;
but the greatest of these is love.

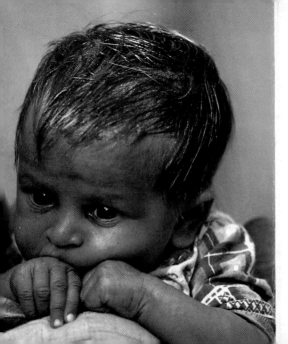

L IFE A FTER D EATH

This is how it will be when the dead are raised to life. When the body is buried, it is mortal; when raised, it will be immortal. When buried, it is ugly and weak; when raised, it will be beautiful and strong. When buried, it is a physical body; when raised, it will be a spiritual body. There is, of course, a physical body, so there has to be a spiritual body.

What is mortal
must be changed into what is immortal.
Then the Scripture will come true
– death is destroyed, victory is complete.

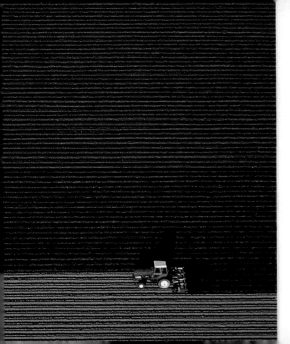

A NEW LIFE

When anyone becomes a Christian, that person is a new being;
the old is gone and the new has come. All this is done by God,
who through Christ changed us from enemies into his friends
and gives us the task of making others his friends also.

I am convinced that neither death nor life, neither angels nor demons, neither the present nor the future, nor any powers, neither height nor depth, nor anything else in all creation, will be able to separate us from the love of God that is in Christ Jesus.

Copyright © 1989 Lion Publishing

Published by
Lion Publishing plc
Icknield Way, Tring, Herts, England
ISBN 0 7459 1404 7 (cased)
ISBN 0 7459 1631 7 (paperback)
Albatross Books Pty Ltd
PO Box 320, Sutherland, NSW 2232, Australia
ISBN 0 86760 953 2 (cased)
ISBN 0 7324 0041 4 (paperback)

First edition 1989

Acknowledgments
All photographs are by Lion Publishing: David Townsend except
Racism and *Life after death* which are by ZEFA (UK) Ltd

Bible quotations are taken from *Good News Bible*, copyright 1966,
1971 and 1976 American Bible Society, published by the Bible
Societies/Collins; *Holy Bible, New International Version* (British
edition) copyright 1978 New York International Bible Society; *Revised
Standard Version*, copyright 1946 and 1952, second edition 1971,
Division of Christian Education, National Council of the Churches of
Christ in the USA

Bible references in the order in which they appear, giving chapt
verse numbers:
The Way to God 1 Corinthians 1:21, 27–29; Romans 11:33
Forgiveness Romans 3:9–12; 3:23–26
Good News Romans 1:16–17; 5:8–9
Equality 1 Corinthians 11:11–12; Galatians 3:28
Racism Romans 10:12–13; Ephesians 2:14, 16
Contentment 1 Timothy 6:6–10; 2 Corinthians 9:8
Peacemaking Romans 12:17–19; 12:20–21
Love 1 Corinthians 13:4–7; 13:13
Life after Death 1 Corinthians 15:42–44; 15:53, 54
A New Life 2 Corinthians 5:17–18; Romans 8:38–39

Printed and bound in Singapore